Tapestry

Tapestry

Entering the Presence of the Lord

KIMBERLY HAUNANI KAY KAU

RESOURCE *Publications* · Eugene, Oregon

TAPESTRY
Entering the Presence of the Lord

Resource Publications
An Imprint of Wipf and Stock Publishers
199 W. 8th Ave., Suite 3
Eugene, OR 97401

www.wipfandstock.com

PAPERBACK ISBN: 978–1–7252–6623–0
HARDCOVER ISBN: 978–1–7252–6624–7
EBOOK ISBN: 978–1–7252–6625-4

01/04/21

This book is dedicated to the memory of a very special woman who helped to shape who I am today, namely my precious mom Wanda Kulamanu Ellis Au.

My beloved mom, you are now smiling down at me as you soar with the angels in heaven.

"I wait for the Lord, my whole being waits,
 and in his word I put my hope."

PSALM 130:5

Contents

Searching;
Finding the Lord Once Again

Redemption and Restoration;
Entering the Presence of the Lord

Preface

This book is designed like a devotional with an original poem, followed by a scripture meditation for deep contemplation on the Lord and his Word.

The topics of the poems vary, but cover a variety of life experiences and emotions which we all face in our daily lives and ongoing challenges.

It is my hope and desire that the poetry in this book will minister deeply to the reader and encourage a more intimate relationship with the Lord as we enter into his glorious presence.

Acknowledgments

This book is a humble offering to my Lord Jesus Christ.

My heartfelt thanks goes first of all to Christ, my Lord and King for loving me unconditionally, and the blessing of this book. Lord, you have encouraged me to daily draw into your presence. I love you Lord.

Wipf and Stock my wonderful publisher who helped to bring this project to completion and publication. Thank you to my fabulous Wipf and Stock team of Matthew Wimer, Caleb Shupe, Savanah N. Landerholm, George Callahan, Zech Mickel and Shannon Carter.

Katie, my beloved daughter for all of your help and support. You are truly my inspiration!

Karl, my dear husband for your lovingly prepared hot meals which sustained me, and the patience and support of my precious family.

My dear dad, Gilbert Kwock On Au for showing me devoted love in staying by mom's side during her long illness.

Thank you to Kea who helped to keep the dream of this book alive.

A big shout-out to my good friends and cheerleaders, namely Patti, Flo, Lisa, Norma, Debbie, Evelyn, the prayer team of Mililani Community Church, and my sister Cecily who believed in me and supported me with your prayers and encouragement.

To my dear friend Amy P. for your wise words of encouragement.

Finally, my gratitude to you, the reader, for opening your heart to the working of the Holy Spirit through the poems and scriptures in this book.

Introduction

I began to write the poems for this book when my precious mom became ill and was diagnosed with a terminal illness eight years ago, so the original poems in this book are very personal to me.

Unfortunately, my dear mom went home to be with the Lord on January 7, 2020.

This book is dedicated in loving memory of her.

I designed this book to invoke deep thought and reflection as you, the reader, finds the poem that would best minister hope to your soul in the situation you are presently facing.

For convenient reference, the poems in this book are divided up into three sections with a different, distinct theme for each section.

The poems in the first section, *Sifting Through Our Emotions and Going Through Difficult Experiences*, address our humanity and the emotions and common experiences that we all go through living in uncertain times and in a fallen world. As I wrote in my poem entitled *Faith*:

> "Faith is allowing the Lord to tightly hold your hand
> Through the dark valleys and the quickening of sand."

The poems in the second section of the book, *Searching; Finding the Lord Once Again*, are contemplative, searching poems, which leads the reader on a journey of seeking, finding, and reflection on the Lord.

> ". . .Turn me again to you and restore me, for you alone are the Lord my God."
> (Jeremiah 31:18)

The poems in the final section of the book, *Redemption and Restoration; Entering the Presence of the Lord*, are poems of restoration and point the reader to the various ways in which our Lord has restored each of our lives to be usable vessels for his glory and for his kingdom.

He is our redeemer! The following excerpt is from my poem *The Shards*:

> "For out of our deepest pain and regret
> All of the issues that we worry about and fret
> Are redeemed by you Lord, as we are made brand new
> Into a beautiful, colorful restored masterpiece with all the bright
> shades of hue."

Sifting Through Our Emotions and Going Through Difficult Experiences

Faith

Faith is the evidence of things not yet seen
Beyond what has been
Trusting the Lord, stepping out, though we cannot always see
All that the Lord has planned for me.
Faith is allowing the Lord to tightly hold my hand
Through the dark valleys and the quickening of sand.

Scripture Meditation:

"Now faith is confidence in what we hope for and assurance about what we
do not see."
(Heb 11:1)

Hope

Hope is hanging on by a thread
Clinging to our faith, instead of to dread.
Hope is believing for the promise of a new tomorrow
Amidst the swirling maze of heartbreak and sorrow.
Our only hope is found in the Lord
In the word which is sharper than any two-edged sword.
Hope enables us to face another day
Confident and secure in the Lord's love that things will be okay.

Scripture Meditation:

"We have this hope as an anchor for the soul, firm and secure. It enters the inner sanctuary behind the curtain, where our forerunner, Jesus, has entered on our behalf. He has become a high priest forever, in the order of Melchizedek."
(Heb 6:19–20)

Love

Love is patient and kind
Love restores, love can bind
Love keeps no record of wrong
Love is the sweet refrain of a song
Love is not rude
Nor is it crude
Love endures through every season of life
Through conflict and even strife.
Love never fails
Love never derails
The Lord's love will endure the test of time and never end
Even a broken heart it can mend
So send some love to someone special today
Love is the answer for this is the Lord's way.

Scripture Meditation:

"And now these three remain: faith, hope and love. But the greatest of these is love."
(1 Cor 13:13)

Kindness

Kindness is doing something nice for a person we don't know
For in due time we will reap what we sow.
A simple kind act can go a long way
Even an encouraging word in what we say
Can lift a person's spirit up and up.
We can be that special person who fills another person's cup
With the Lord's love
Given to us from above.
So share some love and kindness with someone today
Be that bright sunlit ray.

Scripture Meditation:

"Be kind and compassionate to one another, forgiving each other, just as in Christ God forgave you."
(Eph 4:32)

Anger

Dear Lord I feel angry and all alone
But I know that your precious blood shed for me on the cross does atone
For there are things I am going through that I don't understand.
Nevertheless Lord, help me to take a righteous stand
For what is right
We walk by faith and not by sight
Give me calm and peace in my soul
Before all this stress takes a final toll.

Scripture Meditation:

"'In your anger do not sin': Do not let the sun go down while you are still angry, and do not give the devil a foothold."
(Eph 4:26–27)

Fear

Fear can grip your heart
Right from the start
It will stop you in your tracks
Make you more prone to the enemy's attacks.

Fear will give the enemy a foothold
So be bold
When fear strikes, pray
Fill your heart with faith and stay
In what the Lord has in store
For you, the one He will always adore.

Scripture Meditation:

"When I am afraid, I put my trust in you."
(Ps 56:3)

Disappointment

Disappointment leaves us bitterly cold
Dreams that never unfold
Someone's word to us is spoken
Then, a cherished promise is broken.
How it hurts our hearts and makes it ache
Jostles our own spirit awake
Leading us back to the Lord
Who will never forsake.

Scripture Meditation:

"Let us hold unswervingly to the hope we profess, for he who promised is faithful."
(Heb 10:23)

Harpoon

Pointed, sharp barbs, a harpoon
  Aimed directly at my heart, so I retreat
Into my cocoon.
Lord, help me to see
The person I am fighting with is not my enemy.
Every day, we must put on the full armor of God
Then when the insults and criticism
Fly at me like a lightning rod
I will still be able to keep my cool
Instead of acting out like a fool.
Keeping my cool while in the storm
For me, is not the norm
But in the Lord, I shall find my peace while in the fire
So I can persevere and not tire.

Scripture Meditations:

"Finally, be strong in the Lord and in his mighty power. Put on the full armor of God so that you can take your stand against the devil's schemes." (Eph 6:10–11)

Forgiveness

I have been hurt by someone close to me
Unkind words that killed my heart you see.
My first reaction is to get that person back
But this response only shows my personal lack
Of not wanting to let hurt go.
If we don't learn to forgive, the bitterness and anger will only grow
Take root and poison our heart
Keep us apart
Yes, keep us apart
From the one who loves us so
Our Lord who loves us so.

Scripture Meditation:

"Whoever would foster love covers over an offense, but whoever repeats the matter separates close friends."
(Prov 17:9)

Stay

This poem was written in 2015 for my dear brother Brian when he was diagnosed with his rare brain tumor. He survived his brain surgery and subsequent treatments and is cancer free today.

Stay, please stay
Don't go away
I am losing you more with each passing day.
Lord, I wonder if there is any way
To grant us both just one more day.
But, alas the sun has stopped shining
And the shadowy clouds are turning gray
The rain is pouring down
Now, I slowly release you to go and receive your golden crown.

Scripture Meditation:

"For the creation was subjected to frustration, not by its own choice, but by the will of the one who subjected it, in hope that the creation itself will be liberated from its bondage to decay and brought into the freedom and glory of the children of God."
(Rom 8:20–21)

Grief is a Journey

Grief is a journey
A painful road you see
For I am in the midst of my own personal suffering and pain
Tears falling continually from my red, swollen eyes like torrential rain.
I turn to my Lord in order to keep from going insane
I have had to face the cold, hard reality of losing someone I dearly love.
Where is my peace from above?
The acceptance of the loss of my precious mom evades me.
As I struggle and grapple with the Lord I can slowly see
The Lord's loving presence and comfort as the tears fill my eyes once more
Weeping, trembling I am shaken to my inner core.
When we hurt and mourn
The Lord stays by our side and a closer relationship with him is born.
When our anguished hearts are bleeding and shattered in so many pieces
Our dear Lord fills our hearts with comfort and hope when all else in this
chaotic world ceases.

Scripture Meditation:

"The Lord is close to the brokenhearted and saves those who are crushed
in spirit."
(Ps 34:18)

How Can It Be?

How can it be?
My little girl sitting in front of me
Is now all grown up and no longer a child
Independent, with a mind of her own and a streak that is wild.
My heart as a mother laments for gone are the carefree days of playing at the park
Her interests are so different now, markedly stark
As much as I love her with all of my heart
The Lord loves her even more and does not want to be apart.
So, dear Lord please stir up in her a desire
I shall keep praying for her and never tire
For my daughter to know you Lord someday
In order that heaven will be her permanent home to stay.

Scripture Meditation:

"Children are a heritage from the Lord, offspring a reward from him."
(Ps 127:3)

Praise

Praise, praise the Lord!
Let us lift our triumphant voices in one exuberant accord.
Lord, your loving presence is here
Come Lord and fill this place to change the atmosphere
We are not the same
For we shall not live for fortune or fame
Instead we live to exalt the name which is above all names
We shall proclaim!
The wonderful, glorious name of the Lord!

Scripture Meditation:

"It is good to praise the Lord, and make music to your name, O Most High, proclaiming your love in the morning and your faithfulness at night, to the music of the ten-stringed lyre and the melody of the harp."
(Ps 92:1–3)

Pain

Crying, bent over, and sick with excruciating abdominal pain
The pain is now pelting down on my body like sheets of pouring rain.
Unrelenting, pounding, like waves upon the sandy shore
My mind, body, and soul scream out "please Lord, no more, no more!"
In this illness, my whole world has been rocked to the core
Who can I turn to in my deepest time of need?
Only the Lord, and faith is the seed
By which I will believe and receive my total healing of mind, body and soul.
As believers, our faith plays a critical role
In our hardships and difficulties from the past
We must learn to trust the Lord and his precious word for they will ultimately last.

Scripture Meditation:

"I will praise the Lord who counsels me; even at night my heart instructs me. I keep my eyes always on the Lord. With him at my right hand, I will not be shaken."
(Ps 16:7–8)

The Storm

It is very, very late
So late, I have even forgotten today's date.
I am filled with pain, dread and impending doom
We are here as a family at the emergency room.
I am sick with a really bad migraine headache
Dear Lord, it hurts so bad, please do not forsake.
Also, my precious teenage daughter has lost a lot of her blood
Have mercy on her Lord and come like a flood.
Fill me with peace in the midst of the storm
When trusting in you Lord is not the norm
Help me to see in this moment that you know what lies ahead
For I am relying on your word and what you have said.

Scripture Meditation:

"God is our refuge and strength, an ever-present help in trouble."
(Ps 46:1)

Perfect Peace

Lovely, melodious strains wafting in the cool, crisp air
I sit relaxing on a bench beneath the canopy of a large banyan tree
Without one single worry or care.
Lord, the problems of life are often more than we can bear
Sometimes, I don't even know from day to day how I will fare.
But Lord, I am thankful for this blessed moment in time
When I can sit in perfect peace and write this joyful rhyme.

Scripture Meditation:

"You will keep in perfect peace those whose minds are steadfast, because they trust in you! Trust in the Lord forever, for the Lord, the Lord himself, is the Rock eternal."
(Isa 26:3–4)

Joy

A lovely blend of harmonic notes
The meaning that a song denotes
All of the beauty and splendor of emotions it emotes
Is simply . . . joy, so rich and pure . . .
Music is certainly the cure
For whatever ails the mind, body and soul
Melting away all of life's problems which have taken its toll
Like a healing balm
Now a peace and calm
Wash over me.

Scripture Meditation:

"In my distress I called to the Lord; I cried to my God for help. From his temple he heard my voice; my cry came before him, into his ears." (Ps 18:6)

Searching;
Finding the Lord Once Again

Counterfeit

Things may not be as they appear
  So, please steer clear
Of what is not true.
Our faith and the word is the glue
That keeps us on the righteous path, which is good
Our eyes fixed on the Lord and the cross where love once stood.

Scripture Meditation:

"Finally, brothers and sisters, whatever is true, whatever is noble, whatever is right, whatever is pure, whatever is lovely, whatever is admirable—if anything is excellent or praiseworthy—think about such things. Whatever you have learned or received or heard from me, or seen in me—put it into practice. And the God of peace will be with you."
(Phil 4:8–9)

The Egg

I am an egg with a speckled, fragile shell
Made so wonderfully complex, no one can tell.
My white shell is cracked in so many places
Only the Lord can fill all of my empty spaces.
I can be displayed in so many different ways
Depending on the days
I may be hard-boiled or fried,
Tested and tried,
Scrambled, folded into an omelet or even sunny side up.
Lord, please help to fill my empty cup
With your unfailing love
From heaven above.

Scripture Meditation:

"For we are God's handiwork, created in Christ Jesus to do good works, which God prepared in advance for us to do."
(Eph 2:10)

True Colors

Who are we?
Is beyond what the eye can see
We show off what we want to portray
But in the recesses of our hearts, it is like night and day.
Our true intent is buried deep in the heart
But the Lord knows our intentions right from the start.
In a situation rising out of the blue
None of which is true
The ugliness rises in me and in you too.
We can be deceived into thinking we know a person's true intent
Until they suddenly turn on us and leave our hearts with a permanent dent.

Scripture Meditation:

"For the word of God is alive and powerful. Sharper than any double-edged sword, it penetrates even to dividing soul and spirit, joints and marrow; it judges the thoughts and attitudes of the heart. Nothing in all creation is hidden from God's sight. Everything is uncovered and laid bare before the eyes of him to whom we must give account."
(Heb 4:12–13)

Mirror

Mirror, mirror on the wall
Why do you look at your kids with such appall?
What, O Lord is left?
Why do I feel discouraged and bereft?
Do you not know that children are a gift.
Lord, I feel dry. . . I need a spiritual lift
Oh my Lord, fill my cup with your unfailing love
A love as gentle and pure as a dove
Let your living waters flow through me
Until it is only the Lord others see.

Scripture Meditation:

"He heals the brokenhearted and binds up their wounds."
(Ps 147:3)

Reflections

Water flowing and cascading
A continuous, disharmonious cacophony
Plunging downward
Harmonic restitution
As water hits water
Water collides with more water
A circular collection of murky liquid amassed
Amidst slippery, sunken stones.
Searching the cloudy depths of the pool
I cannot see my reflection at the bottom of the pool
But the water looks so inviting, crisp and cool.
Who is that reflection staring back at me?
Only the Lord can truly see.
No eye has ever seen
All of me that could have been
The recesses of my soul now revealed
Even those parts which until now have been carefully concealed.
My heart is now open wide
No longer will I hide.

Scripture Meditation:

"Your eyes saw my unformed body; all the days ordained for me were written in your book before one of them came to be."
(Ps 139:16)

Footprints in the Sand

Footprints displayed in the sand
Deeply embedded, the mark of the Lord's providential hand.
A journey with the Lord depicted within the grains of sand
A medley of moments which include joy mixed with sorrow and moments not so grand.
My Lord, I thought that I was walking through this life all alone
No, no my precious child, you say, I came to atone
For the sins of man
I sent my son Jesus to die in your place.
Now, my beloved daughter, you can see me face to face
Face to face.

Scripture Meditation:

"Those who know your name trust in you for you, Lord,
have never forsaken those who seek you."
(Ps 9:10)

Songbird

I am a songbird in the chilly air
Flying without one single care
With peaceful wings I soar
Your blessings upon me you pour.
Singing a joyful song
Through the dark nights and all the day long
With poetry and musical lore
Your love for me revealed in my inner core.
Precious Lord, what you have placed deep in my heart
Grace and peace O Lord do not depart.

Scripture Meditation:

"Do not be anxious about anything; but in every situation, by prayer and petition, with thanksgiving, present your requests to God. And the peace of God, which transcends all understanding, will guard your hearts and minds in Christ Jesus."
(Phil 4:6–7)

Clouds

White fluffy clouds float casually by
Fill my empty soul Lord for I feel spiritually dry.
You O Lord are my bread of life
Amidst the chaos, struggle and stress of life.
Perfect peace now settles deep in my heart
Lord, my soul and yours can never be apart.
I need your guidance in a choice I must make
I know that whatever choice I make, your love will never forsake.

Scripture Meditation:

"They must turn from evil and do good;
they must seek peace and pursue it."
(1 Pet 3:11)

Grass

I am a blade of grass
Wild and free
But I wonder if you can see
That the wind blows and I am gone.
The start of a new day, the crimson dawn
I turn brown, wither and die
But the love of our Lord rises high, oh so high
Like the fluttering wings of the white butterfly.

Scripture Meditation:

"The life of mortals is like grass,
they flourish like a flower of the field;
the wind blows over it and it is gone,
and its place remembers it no more.
But from everlasting to everlasting the Lord's love is with those who fear
him, and his righteousness with their children's children—
with those who keep his covenant and remember to obey his precepts."
(Ps 103:15–18)

Gaze

I gaze at the stars
Twinkling and blinking in the indigo stained night sky
As I wonder to myself. . .why? Why?
Why do I cry, ponder and deny
The deep despair in my heart.
Where do I start?
The sorrow in my heart will not depart
So I will trust in you Lord with the complexities of my life
Amidst the chaos, stress and strife.
The creator of the universe loves you and me
But why can't I see?
Even the sparrows are under His watchful care
So, don't despair
The Lord knows even the number of hairs on our head
Therefore, I will trust Him, trust Him instead.

Scripture Meditation:

"The Lord is close to the brokenhearted and saves those who are crushed in spirit."
(Ps 34:18)

Rainbow

The beautiful colors of the rainbow
Arching across the blue sky
Rising high, oh so high
Each vibrant color a reflection of what the Lord has made
The sacrificial love that He paid.
A rainbow represents hope for tomorrow
Erasing yesterday's heartbreak and sorrow.

Scripture Meditation:

"Cast your cares on the Lord and he will sustain you; he will never let the righteous be shaken."
(Ps 55:22)

The Leaf

A solitary leaf floating aimlessly to the hard, cracked, acrid ground
Without a single sound
I am like that leaf now in a tailspin
Embroiled in heartbreaking situations that I can't possibly win.
Dearest Lord, I cannot get through all of this alone
But I hear you say to me that your sacrifice on the cross will atone
For all of the anger and sadness dwelling deep within my heart
My only comfort now is to know without a doubt that you O Lord and I will never be apart.

Scripture Meditation:

"May the God of hope fill you with all joy and peace as you trust in him, so that you may overflow with hope by the power of the Holy Spirit."
(Rom 15:13)

The Lone Bird

A solitary bird flying out of sight
Ethereal, soaring, ever so light.
Where can I fly to be away from your attentive eye?
Way, way up yonder in the bluest slice of sky?
O Lord, your loving, caring presence is with me all of the time
Even through my searing pain and all that is sublime.
I will recall that Lord you are good
Let that always be understood.

Scripture Meditation:

"Where can I go from your Spirit?
Where can I flee from your presence?
If I go up to the heavens, you are there;
If I make my bed in the depths, you are there."
(Ps 139:7–8)

Worship Is

Praise the Lord
  Praise the Lord!
Sing out loud in one accord
Let us exalt His name forevermore
In spirit and in truth, from our very core.
For He alone is worthy of our praise
With harmonious voices and with our hands we raise
To our blessed Savior and King
From the earth to the heavens, let our praises exalt and ring.
Let it Ring!

Scripture Meditation:

"It is good to praise the Lord and make music to your name,
O Most High . . ."
(Ps 92:1)

The Sea

The sea, the sea
  Oh, how can it be?
So violent with waves
Then, smooth as glass, that's how it behaves.
But even out here on a ship sailing on the deep blue
The Lord is with me and He is with you too.
I am grateful to you Lord for this wonderful trip
For the chance to relax and for cinnamon tea to sip
Relaxation and time on my side
Time spent with you Lord and time to abide.

Scripture Meditation:

"He says 'Be still and know that I am God.
I will be exalted among the nations, I will be exalted in the earth.'"
(Ps 46:10)

Waves

Waves rolling in from the sea
Like fiery trials headed toward me
Each wave pounding like the surf
Stay away storms, for this is God's turf.

Who do I turn to in my time of need?
The Lord and trust is the seed
By which we will overcome
So we will not be left numb
By the storms of life
which can cut through our lives like a sharp knife.

Scripture Meditation:

"Blessed is the one who perseveres under trial because having stood the test, that person will receive the crown of life that the Lord has promised to those who love him."
(James 1:12)

Motherhood

Motherhood has its valleys and peaks
But through the journey, if we let him the Lord speaks
To our hearts so we can show our children God's love
A love as pure and white as a dove.
Motherhood has its sharp moments of pain
Stress, chaos and even strain.
Motherhood will reveal who we really are
For we know going through life, our Lord is never far.
Motherhood is an opportunity for us to grow
for we will see the fruits in our children of what we sow.

Scripture Meditation:

"Children are a heritage from the Lord,
offspring a reward from him."
(Ps 127:3)

Mom

My dearest Mom, this poem is written for you
You are special to me and I love you too.
Your beauty, grace and optimism unmatched by none
Your unconditional love for me blazing like the noonday sun.
You've taught me so much
About life, marriage, kids and being a mom and such
Thanks for all of the laughs and even a few tears
Through it all, you have helped me remain strong and face my fears.
You taught me to never give up and to see the blessing of each new day
So, my dearest mom to you I say
Our love for each other will never end
For you will always be my best friend.

Scripture Meditation:

"Honor your father and mother—which is the first commandment with a promise . . ."
(Eph 6:2)

Friendship

A true friend is someone who will remain with you through the mountain high and valley low
Someone special in life who will love you unconditionally through the ever changing tide of ebb and flow.

A special friend will reach out to us with an encouraging word, a kind, thoughtful card, or a timely call
Wrapping us securely in heartwarming support when we are ready to fall.

In this life, we are not meant to do this journey all alone
The Lord came down from heaven to atone
For all of the sins of man
Though we once were all sinners and ran
The Lord is our best friend whose love just won't walk away
We can be sure his eternal love will never die and will forever stay.

Scripture Meditation:

"One who has unreliable friends soon comes to ruin,
but there is a friend who sticks closer than a brother."
(Prov 18:24)

Come

Come
Come to me
Can't you see?
I, the Lord will give you sweet rest
For I know what is best
I shall give you peace for your troubled soul
Before all of this stress takes its toll
Just come to me.

Scripture Meditation:

"Set your minds on things above, not on earthly things. For you died, and your life is now hidden with Christ in God."
(Col 3:2–3)

Stuck

I am stuck
In the muck and the mire of life
Swirling amidst the turmoil, stress and strife.
How can I get back on track?
First, I must see all of my lack
My hunger and need
For God, my essential and elemental seed.

Scripture Meditation:

"The Lord is my light and my salvation—
whom should I fear?
The Lord is the stronghold of my life—
of whom shall I be afraid?"
(Ps 27:1)

Secret

I am living in darkness of my sin
Caught deep in a situation I can't win
A deep, dark secret no one can see
But Lord, you still love me, so how can this be?
Lord, help me to do what is right in your eyes
For being honest destroys the enemy's lies.
It is better to have integrity than to be sunken deep in a guise
We honor the Lord in being righteous and wise.

Scripture Meditation:

"Better the poor whose walk is blameless than the rich whose ways are perverse."
(Prov 28:6)

Center

Precious Lord, be the center of my life
Amidst the pressing trials, stress and strife
I open up all areas of my life to you
Have access to heal all the hurts I shall accrue
I cast all of my cares upon you
Take all of these burdens from me
For it is too much for me to bear you see.
Dear Lord, you are still my shepherd and king
Unto you and forever more I will praise you and sing!

Scripture Meditation:

"Cast all your anxiety on him because he cares for you."
(1 Pet 5:7)

Teardrops from Heaven

Teardrops from heaven fall from my eyes
Amidst my sorrow and heartfelt cries
My heart yearns for you Lord my sovereign King
To thee praises I sing
From the ends of the earth let it ring.

Through the storms, trials and pain
Pounding and quiet soft rain
My Lord, growing in trust
Even when my world has turned to dust..

Amidst the chaos, stress and strife
The rubble of my life
A renewed faith in me is born
No more shall I mourn
For whatever the cost
Despite whom I have lost
I will love you Lord
I love you Lord.

Scripture Meditation:

"As the deer pants for streams of water, so my soul pants for you, my God."
(Ps 42:1)

Redemption and Restoration;
Entering the Presence of the Lord

Chains

Our chains
Now the power of the Lord rains
We were bound
Can you hear the sound
Of sweet freedom?
Now our chains are gone
It is the breaking of a brand new dawn
The shackles that were once in our way
Have melted away in the freedom of today.
By the redemptive power of the Lord and the price He paid
The resurrection power of Christ from where He was laid.

Scripture Meditation:

"Therefore if anyone is in Christ, the new creation has come.
The old has gone, the new is here!"
(2 Cor 5:17)

Captive

I am captive
Held fast behind iron clad bars, so I can't live
Stress swirling all around me
Dim and clouded, my spiritual eyes can no longer see..
Dear Lord, there does not seem to be a solution or any relief in sight
For what is happening in this situation is just not right
I need help. . ..Who can help me in my time of need?
Only my Jesus and trust in Him is the seed
By which we will persevere and stand
So that we will not be sucked into deep, despairing quicksand.

Scripture Meditation:

"I lift up my eyes to the mountains—
where does my help come from?
My help comes from the Lord,
the Maker of heaven and earth."
(Ps 121:1–2)

Cracked

I am cracked and broken in so many ways and places
The Lord's refreshing waters filling my empty spaces
Healing, renewing and restoring what the enemy has taken
I am never forgotten by the Lord, nor am I ever forsaken.
My precious Lord, you never waste a hurt in my life
You redeem even the most painful moments of stress and strife
In order to mold me to be more like you
with a pure heart, loving and true.

Scripture Meditation:

"Israel, put your hope in the Lord,
for with the Lord is unfailing love
and with him is full redemption."
(Ps 130:7)

Descent into Darkness

Darkness has crept in descending on my mind and soul
All of this turmoil, stress and strife has finally taken its toll.
Satan, our enemy torments me day and night
Swirling thoughts and threads of anger, turmoil, strife and black fright.
Who can deliver me from evil and encourage me to do good?
My beloved Lord and the hill at Calvary where the cross once stood.

Scripture Meditation:

"So do not throw away your confidence; it will be richly rewarded. You
need to persevere so that when you have done the will of God, you will
receive what he has promised."
(Heb 10:35–36)

Dust

Dearest Lord,
There is nothing left of me
O Lord, can't you see?
In the midst of my extreme suffering, pain and grief
As I desperately sought you for relief
You entered in
My confusion and din
You O Lord breathed new life into my dust
For trust in you is a must.
My life, once a mess of shattered pieces now made whole
For my dearest Lord has restored what the enemy stole.

Scripture Meditation:

"And the God of all grace, who called you to his eternal glory in Christ, after you have suffered a little while, will himself restore you and make you strong, firm and steadfast. To him be the power for ever and ever. Amen." (1 Pet 5:10–11)

Face Down

I fell face down
Silently to the hardened ground.
I could not get up
For bone dry was my spiritual cup.
Lord help me I cried and pleaded looking dejectedly above
When a feeling of divine peace and love as pure as a dove
Descended upon me and gave me the strength I needed in that moment to rise
To reject the enemy's lies
Instead to trust the faithfulness of my beloved Lord, Shepherd and King
Now I can once again hear Heaven rejoice and the angels sing!

Scripture Meditation:

" . . . But those who hope in the Lord
will renew their strength.
They will soar on wings like eagles;
they will run and not grow weary,
they will walk and not be faint."
(Isa 40:31)

Falling

I am going through a terrifying and stressful health trial
Falling backwards down a deep, dark abyss descending rapidly mile after endless mile.

Frightened, lonely, uncertainty eating away at my soul as I crawl through a dark hole

Unrelenting, agonizing pain and suffering now taking its toll.

My only hope is to trust in the Lord alone

His redeeming blood in order to atone

For our sins once scarlet, now white as the driven snow.

Our Lord is the only answer when our lives are laid low

Hope is the silken cord pointing us as believers to our heavenly home

Where we are free at last

From our former lives here on earth and the shackles of our tormenting past.

Scripture Meditation:

"Your Word is a lamp for my feet, a light on my path."
(Ps 119:105)

When Things Go Awry

When things go awry
I could just sit back and sigh
Instead, I must realize that we do not live in a perfect place
For sin has invaded the human race.
Lord, teach me to learn how to offer to others your healing grace
In so doing, we enable others to see the Lord's face.
Lord, make me an instrument of thy perfect peace
Let the lies of the enemy forever more cease.
I desire to be a shining beacon of hope in the dark
Displaying a bright light so stark
The darkness must fade away and out of sight
Leaving only the ebb and flow of soft everlasting light.

Scripture Meditation:

" . . . Because of the tender mercy of our God, by which the rising sun will come to us from heaven to shine on those living in darkness and in the shadow of death, to guide our feet into the path of peace."
(Luke 1:78–79)

The Endless Night

Dark silhouettes and casting shadows shifting in the frightful night
Menacing, hovering, oh, what a loathsome sight!
Until, lo and behold, a bright crack of dawning light
Peeks over the horizon, marking the start of a brand new day
A sliver of hope, within the ever brightening slice of ray.
I can make it through this day
With you Lord by my side to stay.
Here to stay.

Scripture Meditation:

"The Lord has done it this very day; let us rejoice today and be glad."
(Ps 118:24)

Gilroy

Written in memory of the lives lost at the Gilroy garlic festival shooting, Gilroy, California on July 28, 2019.

It was a happy day for a garlic festival at Gilroy
A troubled gunman was on the prowl armed with weapons and an evil ploy.
As his sinister plan unfolded, a number of victims, including an innocent six-year old child were gunned down to the ground
Wordlessly, they crumpled silently without a single sound.
The face of evil had struck without warning with yet another tragic result
Slaying innocent lives now a "normal" societal cult.
Bewilderment, grief and tears sting our cheek
Amidst the hurt and pain, answers that we so desperately seek.
We bring our questions to the only one who can offer us hope
Enabling us to cope
He is Jesus Christ my Lord, who is the same yesterday, today and forevermore
He is knocking at the door
Of your heart.

Scripture Meditation:

"I wait for the Lord, my whole being waits, and in his word I put my hope."
(Ps 130:5)

The Candle

Written in memory of the lives lost in the Las Vegas, Nevada shooting on October 1, 2017.

The lives of the beloved innocent extinguished all too soon
Like the sinking of the silvery lining of the moon
A candle burned out long before its time
With no apparent motive, reason or rhyme.
Our hearts are overwhelmed with grief and loss
We try to cope, weep and at night we even toss
The burning question in all of our minds is "why"?
Why did this happen we wonder, ponder and cry.
Heroes were born on that fateful day
Emerging from the ashes as a bright hope of ray
As the bullets sprayed down with terror from above
Lives were willingly laid down in sacrificial love
The same love that our Lord displayed on the cross
For the Lord is our only hope in times of chaos and loss.
In a world darkened by senseless violence and hate
The uncertainty of life of even our own individual fate
All because a mass murderer has just run amok
We must keep our eyes firmly fixed on Jesus the Rock.

Scripture Meditation:

"And we know that in all things God works for the good of those who love him, who have been called according to his purpose."
(Rom 8:28)

The Railroad Tracks

It seems that in life
Amidst all the stress, chaos and strife
Two railroad tracks of joy and sorrow
Run simultaneously, side by side into the mystery that is tomorrow.
Life is a blend of dark moments and light
Often totally beyond our reach and even our sight.
But our Lord in His infinite, loving wisdom knows just what is up ahead
So let it always be said
We must learn to trust the Lord in the tough times and good
Looking instead to the cross at Calvary where redemption once stood.

Scripture Meditation:

"Do not grieve, for the joy of the Lord is your strength!"
(Neh 8:10)

The River

The river meanders through the winding turns of my life
Coursing, twisting, running wild amidst the daily stress and strife
Leaving broken cisterns in its path, cracked in so many places
God's living waters filling my empty spaces.
The Lord is my source of eternal living waters
Springing forth like a well to quench my deepest thirst
Trickling at first, then bubbling over till I burst
I burst with JOY, the deep longings of my heart
For you and I are no longer apart.

Scripture Meditation:

"Sustain me, my God, according to your promise, and I will live;
do not let my hopes be dashed."
(Ps 119:116)

Light

I wait upon you Lord
I am praying so our hearts will be of one accord
I am sitting here feeling quite bored
Show me Lord what I am moving toward
Help me to trust you Lord, when all the answers I can't see
Strengthen my faith to believe all that can be.
We walk by faith and not by sight
O Lord you are my bright shining light
In a dark world turned away from God
Let my passion and love for you Lord be a lightning rod
To the hurting and lost
No matter the cost.

Scripture Meditation:

"Yes, my soul, find rest in God; my hope comes from him."
(Ps 62:5)

In the Blink of an Eye

In the blink of an eye
I sit down dejectedly and collectively sigh.
Lord, all of the problems that are before me
Are impossible to solve you see.
I need encouragement and hope
The mere ability to cope
With all the swirling chaos, stress and strife
The dusty, scattered ashes of my tattered life
Where does my help come from?
Lord, you are my helper in time of need
So, come Lord
Come.

Scripture Meditation:

"I lift up my eyes to the mountains—
where does my help come from?
My help comes from the Lord,
the Maker of heaven and earth."
(Ps 121:1–2)

Life is a Hill

Life is an unpredictable hill
So, be still
Be still and know that I am God.
When life's tough trials scorch us like a red-hot lightning rod
Our lives are not always on level ground, but contain an array of valleys and peaks
But our loving God is always with each of us who seeks.
God is our refuge in the midst of the tumultuous storm
When shadows of darkness, pain and sorrow appear and form
We can be assured that God will walk by our side and hold our very hand
So that we can daily live for Him, and in every trying circumstance take a righteous stand.

Scripture Meditation

"God is our refuge and strength, an ever-present help in trouble."
(Ps 46:1)

The Light in the Darkness

Jesus, you are my light in the dark
A shining, radiant beam, so bright and stark
You lead us through the perils of the dark and the black torment of night
As we journey through times of trials, tribulations, suffering and fright.
When we are unsure if we can go on and put one foot in front of the other
We will learn to trust in you Lord
For me there is no other
Whose love is closer than a brother.

Scripture Meditation:

"In him was life, and that life was the light of all mankind. The light shines in the darkness, and the darkness has not overcome it."
(John 1:4–5)

Refuge

The Lord is my refuge and my shield
   An invincible armor of protection over me which shall not yield.
In my time of distress, illness and pain
Showering healing comfort from heaven falling like soothing rain
He makes me to lie still in a cool, lush, green, velvety field until I can recover and get well
How long I need to rest there only time will tell.
But my Lord continually looks after me with His tender loving care
Taking all of my burdens upon himself when life seems so unfair.
My beloved shepherd keeps watch over me until I am strong enough to stand on my own two feet
Now healed, whole, strong, and complete.

Scripture Meditation:

"Trust in him at all times you people;
pour out your hearts to him, for God is our refuge."
(Ps 62:8)

Breath

I am sick and in severe respiratory distress
I need air, your loving presence and nothing less.
Lord, be my sweet breath of life
Amidst the chaos, stress and strife
When I thought I couldn't make it through the long watches of the frightful night
You, dear Lord reassured me that we walk by faith and not by sight.
Lord, through the mountain top experiences and valley low
May your peace and love flow
Through me
When I am overwhelmed and it is more than I can bear
You have shown me Lord that you care.

Scripture Meditation:

"Now faith is confidence in what we hope for and assurance about what we do not see."
(Heb 11:1)

A Prayer for Healing

I find myself sick
Heal me Lord and make me whole
Restore unto me what the enemy stole
Heal my mind, body and soul
From this illness that has hit my body and is taking its toll.
Help me to look to you Lord
As my faithful, unshakable healing cord
Knit me back together into one piece
Stronger, wiser without one single crease.
Help others who are not feeling well
To hear your comforting voice as clear as a bell.
Please help me my redeemer and my healing Lord
To meditate on your Word which is sharper than any two-edged sword
This infirmity will not last and shall soon pass away
For only my Lord and your Word shall truly stay.

Scripture Meditation:

"Praise the Lord, my soul, and forget not all his benefits—
who forgives all your sins and heals all your diseases . . ."
(Ps 103:2–3)

The Healing Pool

The healing pool
Sparkles with crystal clear waters so cool
I step into the water to receive healing of my mind, body and soul
My infirmity has wracked my body with pain and is insidiously taking a
heavy toll.
But our renewed and matured faith in God plays a vital role
In our healing
For we need to thwart what the enemy is stealing.
Our golden cord of eternal hope
Is our lifeline as believers in Christ, our very rope
Transporting us to the heavenly throne of grace
And our precious Lord's beautiful, beaming face.

Scripture Meditation:

"Praise our God, all peoples, let the sound of his praise be heard;
he has preserved our lives and kept our feet from slipping."
(Ps 66:8–9)

Greeting the Dawn

A slim sliver appears on the horizon as the cracking dawn of light
Is now finally within my sight
In my serious illness, the good Lord has taken me through the long watches
Of the painful, dark night
Enduring the shadow of terror, uncertainty and ominous fright.
Renewed gratitude erupts in my now hopeful heart
For I realize that the Lord's love for me will never depart
It shall never depart.

Scripture Meditation:

"Jesus Christ is the same yesterday and today and forever."
(Heb 13:8)

The Juggler

Lord, I am a juggler with so many balls in the air
Please take all of my problems and cares
Day by day, I am carefully trying to balance each colorful airborne ball
But alas, they are now getting ready to fall
To the ground
With a loud, clattering sound.
In this life, I am way too busy
So many challenges and responsibilities each day has made my head dizzy
I am overwhelmed by all that I have to do
But why just sit here and stew.
Today, I am extra busy wearing a multicolored, rainbow hat on my head
Help me Lord to keep my eyes fixed on you instead.

Scripture Meditation:

"Cast all your anxiety on him because he cares for you."
(1 Pet 5:7)

The Cave

When we are afraid to step out, worried that we might fail
When the mountain that looms before us seems too steep to scale
When the opportunity has slipped away and the boat is ready to sail
When we are up to our necks in trouble and anxiety makes us want to bail
We find ourselves hiding in a cave from life
All of its obstacles, stress and strife.
But alas the Lord can do his best work in molding and shaping a human heart
In order to set us apart
For it is when we are hidden in the cave that the Lord can resurrect dead things
So we can receive all of the Lord's blessings that he brings.

Scripture Meditation:

"Bring an end to the violence of the wicked, and make the righteous
secure—you, the righteous God who probes minds and hearts.
My shield is God Most High, who saves the upright in heart."
(Ps 7:9–10)

The Cry—A Prayer

Dear Lord,
In my searing physical pain, I cried out in desperation for your aid
But you turned your face from me and instead said
Your sins are washed white as snow and are fully paid
They were nailed to the cross at Calvary where I was laid
I, the Lord know that your heart is broken and you wonder
My child, lay all your fears and doubts asunder.
I am with you now and forever more
Receive your healing by the stripes upon me which I bore
I bore
I love you. . . let it sink deep into your spirit and into the depths of your core.

Scripture Meditation:

"He himself bore our sins in his body on the cross,
so that we might die to sins and live for righteousness;
by His wounds you have been healed."
(1 Pet 2:24)

The Valley

The deep, dark cavernous valley beckons and calls
Beckons and calls
Blanketed with blistery trials when all that is familiar falls.
It is a comfort to feel the Lord's abiding presence at my side
So I can face my giants with courage, instead of hide.
In life, we cannot always remain on the exultation of the mountaintop
For continuing trials cause us to pause and to stop.
But the Lord is faithful to us in the good times and bad
Through all the strains of joy and even bellowing sad.
His love is constant and will not let us go
Enabling us to defeat our enemy, our greatest foe.

Scripture Meditation:

"In all this you greatly rejoice, though now for a little while you may had
had to suffer grief in all kinds of trials. These have come so that the proven
genuineness of your faith—of greater worth than gold, which perishes
even though refined by fire—may result in praise, glory and honor when
Jesus Christ is revealed."
(1 Pet 1:6–7)

Rolling

Waves rolling like curves upon the sand
Turning, frolicking, cascading until they reach land
Like the events that roll unexpectedly into our lives
Along with the pain and suffering it derives.
We can barely make sense of it all
As we strive to follow the Lord daily and answer His call
We must find the strength to run the race, stay the course and hold fast
By looking ahead to the bright future the Lord has for each of us and not looking to our past.

Scripture Meditation:

"I have fought the good fight, I have finished the race,
I have kept the faith."
(2 Tim 4:7)

The Return

Dear Lord,
I have drifted away
Lead me back to trust you and obey
My world is falling apart
For the enemy has wounded me with his strategic dart.
By faith, I believe that you care for me
Help me to be patient to wait to see all that can be.
We walk by faith and not by sight
Not by power, not by might
But by my spirit says the Lord.
So, if you are struggling today in your walk with the Lord
Pray to God and meditate on his Word which is sharper than
any two-edged sword.
When we return to God, he waits with open arms of love
Angels rejoice and all of heaven above.

Scripture Meditation:

"Let us hold unswervingly to the hope we profess, for he who promised is faithful."
(Heb 10:23)

Reborn

I am worn
Bone weary, my heart grieving and torn
Tattered, shattered, battered and shorn.
Jesus my Lord you took my sin, shame, and scorn
Upon your shoulders on the cross so I could be reborn
I will no longer mourn or feel forlorn
I have been reborn
REBORN!

Scripture Meditation:

"Now to him who is able to do immeasurably more than all we ask or imagine, according to his power that is at work within us, to him be glory in the church and in Christ Jesus throughout all generations, for ever and ever! Amen."
(Eph 3:20–21)

The Peace of God

The eternal peace of God
Ushered deep into my heart like a piercing lightning rod.
Your peace is like a warm golden ray of light
Contrasting against the backdrop of the dark, frightful night
Enabling me to endure the tough circumstances before me
Faith now rising, rising letting me see
The Lord himself directs the very path I am on
Like the rising of the crimson dawn.

Scripture Meditation:

"For you, God, tested us; you refined us like silver.
You brought us into prison and laid burdens on our backs.
You let people ride over our heads; we went through fire and water,
but you brought us to a place of abundance."
(Ps 66:10–12)

Turning Around

Sometimes in life we find ourselves headed down the wrong road
Heavily burdened and carrying a troublesome load.
The Lord can help us to take a complete U-turn
Follow His path instead and nurture our minds to learn.
We may be stubborn and want to press on through the blockade
Instead of humbling ourselves before the Lord and seeking His wise aid
We resist turning around
As we mistakenly think that our own judgement is sound.
But the thoughts and ways of the Lord are righteous and true
He knows what is best for me and for you.

Scripture Meditation:

"In their hearts humans plan their course, but the Lord establishes their steps."
(Prov 16:9)

Precious

I am precious in his sight
And to the Lord's great delight
By the power of his glorious might
Now I am free to be the salt and light
In this dark and dying world for all to see
For I am truly unique, special, wonderful and free to be
All that the good Lord has in his special plans for me.

Scripture Meditation:

"For you created my inmost being; you knit me together in my mother's womb.
I praise you because I am fearfully and wonderfully made; your works are wonderful, I know that full well."
(Ps 139:13–14)

The Wine of God

I am a grape unblemished, untarnished and whole without a trial or soul
Suddenly, the fiery furnace of life's trials crushes me leaving a gaping hole.
Indeed, it is a sign
That I cannot be poured out wine
If I remain a whole grape.
For under the weight of being tested and tried under fire
If I keep my faith and don't tire
The sweetness and aroma of the grape will be turned into a beautiful fruity wine
Now transformed into a usable vessel from the one who is the true vine
Jesus Christ!

Scripture Meditation:

"But the plans of the Lord stand firm forever, the purposes of his heart through all generations."
(Ps 33:11)

Love Came Down

Love came down from heaven at Christmas time
Through the fog of this sinful world and all that is sublime
A precious gift sent straight from the heart of God
His beloved son, the baby Jesus, born humbly in a manger among sheep and sod.
Conceived in everlasting love to save us all
So we could have a personal relationship with him and answer the call
Jesus Christ is my Bright Morning Star, Everlasting Father, Prince of Peace
Now the grip of sin and death shall forever more cease.

Scripture Meditation:

"For to us a child is born,
to us a son is given,
and the government will be on his shoulders.
And he will be called
Wonderful Counselor, Mighty God,
Everlasting Father, Prince of Peace."
(Isa 9:6)

Christmas Peace

The lovely song of the chorale emotes its perfect harmonic notes
Peace, harmony and a heavenly melody it denotes
Melting, silky, a healing balm for the troubled heart and soul
Stress dissipates which had been taking its toll
On Me.
Oh Lord, why can't you see?
I am at my wits end
Peace and healing for my broken, shattered soul please send
Minister to my heart and attend.
Where can we find hope
When we are at the end of our rope?
Love came down from heaven at Christmas time
Silently, God's amazing love burst forth so sublime
The little baby Christ child born on Christmas day
Our Lord is here to stay.

Scripture Meditation:

"You are the God who performs miracles;
you display your power among the peoples."
(Ps 77:14)

He Is Here

Thank you Lord for a Savior is born in Bethlehem today
In the humble manger where the Christ child lay
Hope, yes sweet hope for a desperate and dying world that has gone astray
My Lord Jesus Christ is here to stay.
Now I can bravely face the challenges of a brand new day
Though honestly, I have no idea what troubling situation is barreling straight my way
My world is crumbling as the dawn of the horizon is slowly turning gray
But come Lord, I need you, so please return to earth without delay.

Scripture Meditation:

"He died for us so that, whether we are awake or asleep,
we may live together with him.
Therefore encourage one another and build each other up,
just as in fact you are doing."
(1 Thess 5:10–11)

The Bridge

Dearest Jesus,
You stretched out your broken and bloodied body and became a bridge
at Golgotha, upon that old rugged cross on a desolate ridge.
The Lord is the sacrificial lamb, who was laid out between God and man
enabling us to find salvation so that we can
see our precious Lord face to face.
As believers, we now take our rightful place
Sweet bye and bye
Take me to my heavenly home in the sky
For all of eternity.

Scripture Meditation:

"I am the good shepherd. I know my sheep, and my sheep know me—just
as the Father knows me and I know the Father—and I lay down my life for
the sheep."
(John 10:14–15)

The Quilt

The family of God resembles the assorted patches of a colorful quilt
The individual squares of different colors and patterns upon which the quilt
Is built
A solitary square standing alone
Individually sewn
May find it difficult to stand on its own;
but when the Lord, the Master Quilter,
carefully puts all the patches together in stitch
Our lives collectively linked together in order to enrich
The result is a beautiful, colorful tapestry, a true masterpiece
Perfectly in unison, without one single crease.

Scripture Meditation:

"Now you are the body of Christ, and each of you is a part of it."
(1 Cor 12:27)

For All Time

Dearest Lord, my Savior, you died for me on the cross
And changed the world for all of time
Took every one of my sins and every crime
Upon your shoulders went our crimson stains and our shame
For our redemption is why you came.
The richest love displayed on a wooden cross for all to see
But it was love that kept you there, oh how can it be?
Once and for all, the price for me was paid
Our majestic Lord was resurrected from where He was laid.
Hallelujah! Praise the Lord! You are alive
Hallelujah! for our heavenly home we will someday arrive.

Scripture Meditation:

"But because of his great love for us, God, who is rich in mercy, made us alive with Christ even when we were dead in transgressions—it is by grace you have been saved."
(Eph 2:4–5)

It Was For Me

It was for me Jesus that you died
Willingly laid down your life with one final breath and sigh
Your words uttered on the cross "It is finished" for all time
Upon your shoulders were heaped every one of our sins, our shame, and every crime
At Golgotha on a desolate hill
Time forever stood still
As you suffered agony on that wooden cross for me
The purest love displayed for all to see.
Jesus, the forces of hell came at you from every conceivable side
But your ultimate sacrifice turned the tide
Our sins went from scarlet to white
Darkness was vanquished, our eyes opened wide with new sight.
Jesus Christ is the same yesterday, today and forevermore
Because of the nails in your hands and in your feet that you bore.

Scripture Meditation:

"Therefore we do not lose heart. Though outwardly we are wasting away, yet inwardly we are being renewed day by day. For our light and momentary troubles are achieving for us an eternal glory that far outweighs them all." (2 Cor 4:16–17)

God Cries

Thunderbolts rumble from far away
Strikes of lightning seem here to stay
The rain pours down upon the quaking earth
Anguished screams from heaven as God cries
As he watches his beloved son Jesus cry out, be tortured, then dies.
Why?
Because God gave His only begotten son so that sin would be vanquished
Death overcome
Not for some, but for all of mankind.

Scripture Meditation:

"For God so loved the world that he gave his one and only Son,
that whoever believes in him shall not perish but have eternal life."
(John 3:16)

He Paid It All

Jesus paid it all
By answering His Heavenly Father's call
Jesus paid my debt
My sin and punishment on the cross Christ met.
As Jesus died on the cross, his blood ran red
But, three days later Jesus was raised from the dead
Sin had left a crimson stain
By Jesus's sacrifice, we are washed white as snow and renewed like the cleansing of falling rain.

Scripture Meditation:

"Therefore, if anyone is in Christ, the new creation has come:
The old has gone, the new is here!"
(2 Cor 5:17)

Hallelujah

Hallelujah, all praise to our King
Let the sweet melody of our song ring
Throughout this dark and fallen land
May the providential hand
Of Christ heal every broken heart and see every tear shed
By the power of Christ's blood running red.

Scripture Meditation:

"Record my misery;
list my tears on your scroll—
are they not in your record?"
(Ps 56:8)

The Rack

I see the whip as lashes were viciously laid down upon your back
Bruised and bloodied, like raw meat exposed and laying upon a rack.
You took the stripes for me, in order that I may not lack
A personal relationship with my Savior and Lord
Now, my heart is forever intertwined with yours in one heavenly accord.

Scripture Meditation:

"But he was pierced for our transgressions, he was crushed for our
iniquities; the punishment that brought us peace was on him,
and by his wounds we are healed."
(Isa 53:5)

Hurricane

Sometimes our lives are like the massive, swirling eye of a hurricane-like storm
Where everything is not as it should be, is totally shattered, and is not the norm.
The Lord is our peace in the midst of the calm eye surrounded by ferocious, beating wind and rain
When our hearts are shattered with unrelenting, insidious raw pain.
The Lord can be trusted to take us safely through the storm to the other side
Where the storm can subside, leaving only the ebb and ripple of tide.
Our beloved Lord and shepherd leads us to a place of restful green
A beautiful place of renewal beyond which no eye has seen.

Scripture Meditation:

"He makes me lie down in green pastures,
he leads me beside quiet waters . . ."
(Ps 23:2)

Tapestry

Jesus the weaver expertly crafts the tapestry of my life
   Amidst the trials, stress and strife
Each colorful thread put into its proper place
Even the dark moments of life that we ultimately face
Fibers skillfully woven with a purpose and a plan
For each of our lives
Even though it may seem that only pain and suffering it derives.
We can only see a portion of what Jesus is crafting day by day
But if we learn to trust Jesus and his glorious way
In the end, we will be his beautiful masterpiece
Without one single fold or crease.

Scripture Meditation:

"And we know that in all things God works for the good of those who love
him, who have been called according to his purpose."
(Rom 8:28)

The Broken Shell

I am a beautiful, colorful, uniquely made, broken shell
Oh, but how can anyone tell?
I lay on the white, sandy shore
Oh, but there is so much more.
On the outside, I may look put together and whole
But on the inside, I am hurting and shattered from what the enemy stole
In the recesses of my fragile soul, who I am is hidden deep inside
Revealed only by the gentle erosion of ripple and tide.
How can the Lord use a broken shell?
Broken shells mean the shedding of anguished tears
Daily facing my fears
Torrential heart-wrenching pain
Pouring and pelting down like cascading rain.
Broken shells encourage others to not give up
By turning to the Lord to fill their empty cup
Broken shells are shells that have been tested by fire
They are shells that may grow weary, but do not tire.
Broken shells are shells that have been tried, but never quit
Now refined to emit
Faith and hope for a brighter day
Warmed by the sun's brightest slice of ray.

Scripture Meditation:

"My comfort in my suffering is this:
Your promise preserves my life."
(Ps 119:50)

The Calendar

I received my beautiful wall calendar in the mail
It took a long, long time to get here, slow as a snail.
Oh my goodness, the calendar pages are dented and bent
Though there is still beauty in it and a charm that it lent.
We are like that calendar; our pages are not smooth, but bent and have creases
But with the Lord's atoning sacrifice, our creases ceases.
His blood washes all our sins away
Come what may.
The Lord does not discard us or toss us away
His holy sacrifice from the tomb where he lay.
The Lord fills our blank pages with all that is good
From the hill at Calvary where the wooden cross once stood.

Scripture Meditation:

"But because of his great love for us, God, who is so rich in mercy, made us alive with Christ even when we were dead in transgressions—it is by grace you have been saved."
(Eph 2:4–5)

The Shards

Dear Lord. . . today a ceramic bowl fell from my slippery hands onto the cold, hard kitchen tile floor.

It startled and stressed me and shook me to the core.

With dismay, I gazed at the dozens of pieces cracked beyond repair

for all I could do was simply stare.

Suddenly, my eyes were open and I could see

A spiritual lesson being taught to me.

Lord, you take the fractured pieces of my own life

Amidst all of the chaos, stress and strife

You endow me with your precious hope

Plus the ability to cope.

For out of our deepest pain and regret

All of the issues that we worry about and fret

Are redeemed by you Lord, as we are made brand new

Into a beautiful, colorful restored masterpiece with all the bright shades of hue.

Scripture Meditation:

"He will yet fill your mouth with laughter and your lips with shouts of joy."
(Job 8:21)

The Story

I wish I were the author of my own life story
But it is not about me; rather it is all for His glory.

For it is the Lord himself who is the author and finisher of each chapter of our life

Amidst all of the stress, chaos, and strife.

Each chapter carefully crafted by our Lord with great attention to detail

In order that we as believers keep on the narrow path which will enable us to not derail.

Certainly in our lives, the individual characters, and twisting and turning plot

May not at all be what we sought

However, we continue on with courage in our hearts as we know the good story ending leading to victorious hope

All of which enables us to cope.

Scripture Meditation:

"Therefore, since we are surrounded by such a great crowd of witnesses, let us throw off everything that hinders and the sin that so easily entangles. And let us run with perseverance the race marked out for us, fixing our eyes on Jesus, the pioneer and perfecter of faith. For the joy set before him he endured the cross, scorning its shame, and sat down at the right hand of the throne of God."
(Heb 12:1–2)

Diamond

Jesus, the master jewel maker
Takes our many facets
Considers our weaknesses and our assets
Polishes and buffs away our every flaw
Takes our hurt and our searing pain, no matter how inflamed or raw
Transforming us into a new, beautiful sparkling gem.
Jesus is holding us in his open arms of love, never to condemn
Behold, the sacrificial lamb who was slain
In order that salvation we may obtain.

Scripture Meditation:

"Therefore, there is now no condemnation for those who are in Christ Jesus, because through Christ Jesus the law of the Spirit who gives life has set you free from the law of sin and death."
(Rom 8:1–2)

The Composer

Dearest Lord,
Help me not to forget that my precious life is a song
And most importantly that all along
You O Lord are the master composer and conductor who brings together the harmonic notes of my life
Amidst all of the stress, turmoil and unending strife.
The major uplifting notes in my life play a key role
When life begins to take its toll
But it is actually the discordant melody played in the minor key that draw us closer to the Lord's heart
So that our heart can be in tune with the Lord's heart and never be apart
From the one who loves each of us with an unfailing love
Straight from the heavenly throne above.

Scripture Meditation:

"Then Jesus came to them and said, 'All authority in heaven and on earth has been given to me. Therefore, go and make disciples of all nations, baptizing them in the name of the Father and of the Son and of the Holy Spirit, and teaching them to obey everything I have commanded you. And surely I am with you always, to the very end of the age.'"
(Matt 28:18–20)

The Master Carver

Jesus the carver chisels away in us all that is not pleasing to Him
For we are his precious people, blocks of rough wood that he will trim.
But first we must allow Jesus to come into our lives in order to cut, sand and shape where he will
This refiner's process can often be painful, so we must learn to be still
For hidden beneath the lumps of uncarved wood lies our knots, jagged twigs, and bark
Waiting to be molded into a beautiful masterpiece so stark
In contrast to what we were before
Now, our redeemer Jesus Christ will restore.

Scripture Meditation

"This is how we know that we live in him and he in us:
He has given us of his Spirit."
(1 John 4:13)

The Potter

Jesus the master potter takes a lump of clay which represents our life
Amidst the stress, chaos, heartbreak and strife.
He skillfully shapes and trims the lopsided clay, then we are placed in an oven to be fired up
It is in the red hot kiln that all excess clay is burned away, and what is left is gently placed in a special individual cup.
Jesus then paints us with a special coat of glaze
For all of our days
We now bear the seal of the potter's righteous right hand
Our lives now beautiful treasured vessels, like the grains of sand.
An incomplete masterpiece, as we are all still in the process of change
which can range
Day by day
Our lives an assorted array
Of joy, pain, heartbreak and sorrow
But the potter's capable, sovereign hands holds the mystery that is tomorrow.

Scripture Meditation:

"Yet you, Lord, are our Father.
We are the clay, you are the potter;
we are all the work of your hand."
(Isa 64:8)

The Painting

God is the divine restorer of our lives
The canvas displaying an array of dark and light shades of paint
For each and every one of us as believers are his precious saint.
With each carefully crafted stroke
God will evoke
Born out of our distressing circumstances and pain
Our invaluable gain
A deeper faith, richer maturity, pure beauty and spiritual insight
Bringing forth hope and eternal light
Molding us more into the image of his son
The will of the Father in our lives now done.

Scripture Meditation:

"The Lord has heard my cry for mercy;
the Lord accepts my prayer."
(Ps 6:9)

Mosaic

Jesus the master craftsman meticulously and with purpose puts together
the colorful mosaic tiles of my life
Amidst the chaos, stress and strife.
Each tile carefully put into its proper place
Building all along my Christian race
Even the dark colored tiles have a purpose and a plan when we can't make sense of it
Jesus in His perfect divine wisdom reveals His purpose bit by bit
Uncovering slowly only what we need to know
In order that we as Christians may mature and grow.
If we put our trust in Jesus and his divine way
Day by day
Our lives will be a sacred, beautiful masterpiece on display
A masterpiece without one single fold or crack
Only sweet perfection, without any lack.

Scripture Meditation:

". . . Being confident of this, that he who began a good work in you will carry it on to completion until the day of Christ Jesus."
(Phil 1:6)

Mountaintop

Lord, a mountain looms in front of me
It is just too hard for me to scale you see.
But I don't do this journey alone
The seeds of faith that were planted in me and sown
Will help me to climb up and up to the very top.
Therefore, I will not stop
Lord, with you by my side
Your comforting voice whispering to me "Abide, abide"
My journey is now complete and I am home at last
The pain and sorrow of this life are now in my past
Behold a new light beckons and calls.

Scripture Meditation:

"I consider that our present sufferings are not worth comparing with the glory that will be revealed in us."
(Rom 8:18)

The Hole

Dearest Lord,
I am at home under quarantine
I feel alone and trapped, as if in a deep, dark hole.
Restore my broken, sad spirit, and body, which the enemy stole
Bring forth fresh peace and healing and allow joy to flood my thirsty soul
For all the uncertainty, stress, and chaos have all taken its toll.
Reveal to me the importance of keeping my enduring faith and its role
Centering my heart, mind, and soul
On my one main goal
To live every day of my life for you Lord
Now my will and yours precious Lord are of one accord.

Scripture Meditation:

"No, in all these things we are more than conquerors through him who loved us.
For I am convinced that neither death nor life, neither angels nor demons, neither the present nor the future, nor any powers, neither height nor depth, nor anything else in all creation, will be able to separate us from the love of God that is in Christ Jesus our Lord."
(Rom 8:37–39)

Someday

Written on Easter Sunday 2020.

Someday, someday I will truly and happily say
There will be no more pandemic coming our way.
But for now I say with such dismay
The clouds are turning a dusty shade of gray
For there is no semblance of light or slice of ray
As this deadly Covid19 virus is on the rampage and is not yet kept at bay
There seems to be no way.
So please come quickly Lord Jesus without delay
To our collapsing world now encapsulated with death and decay
Our only hope is in the Lord who is risen today!

Scripture Meditation:

"Praise be to the Lord,
for he has heard my cry for mercy.
The Lord is my strength and my shield;
my heart trusts in him, and he helps me.
My heart leaps for joy,
and with my song I praise him."
(Ps 28:6–7)

Time

Time, like the grains of sand
   Slipping through our hand
Held fast it cannot be
Because you see
The Lord is the keeper of time.
As the years climb
Our past, present and what is to come
May be scary to some
But if we trust the Lord with what is ahead
Then let it always be said
We shall not fear what cannot be seen
Even when times are lean.
The Lord holds us each in the palm of His loving hand
For when our time here is over
It is in heavenly eternity we shall stand.

Scripture Meditation:

"The Lord will keep you from all harm—
he will watch over your life;
the Lord will watch over your coming
and going both now and forevermore."
(Ps 121:7–8)

The Bride and the Groom

The Lord covers us in his love
A love as pure and as gentle as a dove
For he laid down his life for me
His sacrificial love unfailing you see
A love that will not change; a love that won't let us down
His beautiful bride displaying her eternal gown.
We are to love in the same way
A portrait of selfless, unconditional love on display
For all the world to see
A vessel of the Lord's love we shall be.

Scripture Meditation:

"Now that you have purified yourselves by obeying the truth so that you have sincere love for each other, love one another deeply, from the heart." (1 Pet 1:22)

My Song of Inspiration

The Lord's strength and shield
Are an invincible armor which shall not yield.
I see his face with unconditional love
With beauty, grace and affection granted from above.

The seeds of faith grow into a tree
With fruits of integrity for mankind to see.
This tree, a person of the Lord's will
Faith and obedience it shall fulfill.

Precious Lord, Creator and great Physician heals the ill
Mending mind, body and soul for it is his will.
The Lord understands our hurt and pain
He lends a comforting hand soft as rain.

Life was his precious gift
So, why are there so many lives adrift?
The Lord wants us to love
To be as free and as pure as a dove.
Just as a tree moves and bends
So must we to make amends.

Redeemer, Savior, Friend
There to attend
Showered by his tender loving care
When we are burdened by more than we can bear.
The Lord, our Shepherd leads the flock
Let Him into your heart when you hear His knock.
The gates of Heaven are open to you
If you love the Lord with all of your heart
And know that what He wants is true.

Scripture Meditation:

"The Lord is my light and my salvation—whom shall I fear? The Lord is
the stronghold of my life—of whom shall I be afraid?"
(Ps 27:1)

Heaven

Sweet bye and bye
Sweet bye and bye
In the blink of an eye
We are strangers passing through on our way home to our
Eternal mansion in the sky.
In heaven, no more shall we cry
For every single tear he shall wipe dry
The sorrow and suffering of this life shall be passed away
It shall no longer stay.
Our pain-wracked bodies shall be made brand new
More marvelous and glorious than the body we once knew.
Well done my good and faithful servant says the Lord
For all of us as believers shall now be of one accord
No more discord, no more stress
Only perfection, harmony, peace and nothing less.

Scripture Meditation:

"'He will wipe every tear from their eyes. There will be no more death or mourning or crying or pain, for the old order of things has passed away.'" (Rev 21:4)

"Rejoice always, pray continually,
give thanks in all circumstances,
for this is God's will for you in Christ Jesus."

1 Thessalonians 5:16–18

www.ingramcontent.com/pod-product-compliance
Lightning Source LLC
Chambersburg PA
CBHW071131090426
42736CB00012B/2087